Dashing
Dragonflies

Mary Elizabeth Salzmann

Consulting Editor, Diane Craig, M.A./Reading Specialist

A Division of ABDO

ABDO
Publishing Company

visit us at www.abdopublishing.com

Published by ABDO Publishing Company, a division of ABDO, P.O. Box 398166, Minneapolis, Minnesota 55439. Copyright © 2012 by Abdo Consulting Group, Inc. International copyrights reserved in all countries. No part of this book may be reproduced in any form without written permission from the publisher. SandCastle™ is a trademark and logo of ABDO Publishing Company.

Printed in the United States of America, North Mankato, Minnesota
102011
012012

 PRINTED ON RECYCLED PAPER

Editor: Katherine Hengel
Content Developer: Nancy Tuminelly
Cover and Interior Design and Production: Kelly Doudna, Mighty Media, Inc.
Photo Credit: Shutterstock

Library of Congress Cataloging-in-Publication Data

Salzmann, Mary Elizabeth, 1968-
 Dashing dragonflies / Mary Elizabeth Salzmann.
    p. cm. -- (Bug books)
 ISBN 978-1-61783-190-4
 1. Dragonflies--Juvenile literature. I. Title.
 QL520.S25 2012
 595.7′33--dc23
                    2011023251

SandCastle™ Level: Transitional

SandCastle™ books are created by a team of professional educators, reading specialists, and content developers around five essential components—phonemic awareness, phonics, vocabulary, text comprehension, and fluency—to assist young readers as they develop reading skills and strategies and increase their general knowledge. All books are written, reviewed, and leveled for guided reading, early reading intervention, and Accelerated Reader® programs for use in shared, guided, and independent reading and writing activities to support a balanced approach to literacy instruction. The SandCastle™ series has four levels that correspond to early literacy development. The levels are provided to help teachers and parents select appropriate books for young readers.

Emerging Readers
(no flags)

Beginning Readers
(1 flag)

Transitional Readers
(2 flags)

Fluent Readers
(3 flags)

Contents

Dashing Dragonflies 4

Find the Dragonfly 22

Glossary 24

Dashing Dragonflies

Dragonflies have long, thin bodies. Their bodies look striped.

Dragonflies are very colorful.
Some have **fancy designs.**

A dragonfly has very big eyes.
They look like a helmet.

Dragonflies have two **antennae**.
They are very small.

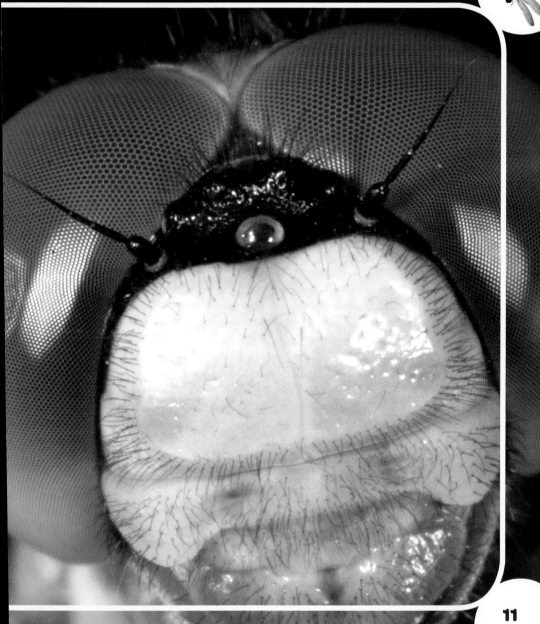

Dragonflies have four large wings. You can see through them.

Dragonflies can fly **forward, backward**, up, down, and sideways.

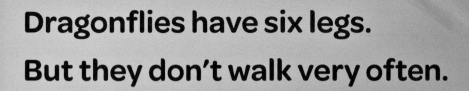

Dragonflies have six legs.
But they don't walk very often.

Dragonflies eat other **insects**. They hold their food with their legs.

19

Dragonflies live near rivers, streams, lakes, and ponds.

Find the Dragonfly

A

B

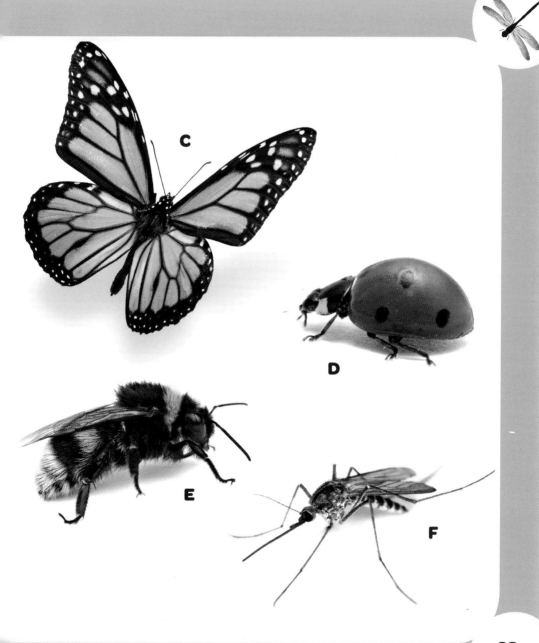

C

D

E

F

Glossary

antenna – a feeler on an insect's head.

backward – behind, or toward the back.

design – a decorative pattern.

fancy – decorative or pretty. Not plain.

forward – ahead, or toward the front.

insect – a small creature with two or four wings, six legs, and a body with three sections.

sideways – to or from the side.